Nikki Carmody is a single parent to five children and lives in the UK. She used to love life with a passion, up until four years ago when she was diagnosed with emotional personality disorder and then shortly after, bipolar disorder. Life since has proven extremely difficult as she has an average of one psychotic episode every couple of months. Each one can last between two and four days, and can be described as 'the worst feeling in the world'.

Over time, Nikki noticed family friends and others not listening to her, not because they are rude, but because they simply don't understand. She feels that no one does and that to most people, she simply comes across as crazy. This is what inspired her to stop talking to others and instead put her thoughts and feelings on paper.

Far from an expert writer, these are all genuine thoughts and feelings mixed with emotion, resulting in poems that will hopefully help you feel a little comfort, knowing that someone else out there is going through the same thing.

Nikki Carmody

BIPOLAR ROLLERCOASTER

AUSTIN MACAULEY PUBLISHERS™
LONDON • CAMBRIDGE • NEW YORK • SHARJAH

Copyright © Nikki Carmody 2024

The right of Nikki Carmody to be identified as author of this work has been asserted by the author in accordance with sections 77 and 78 of the Copyright, Designs and Patents Act 1988.

All rights reserved. No part of this publication may be reproduced, stored in a retrieval system, or transmitted in any form or by any means, electronic, mechanical, photocopying, recording, or otherwise, without the prior permission of the publishers.

Any person who commits any unauthorised act in relation to this publication may be liable to criminal prosecution and civil claims for damages.

A CIP catalogue record for this title is available from the British Library.

ISBN 9781528918343 (Paperback)
ISBN 9781528962278 (ePub e-book)

www.austinmacauley.co.uk

First Published 2024
Austin Macauley Publishers Ltd®
1 Canada Square
Canary Wharf
London
E14 5AA

Table of Contents

One Wish	9
A Mother's Love	10
Love Hurts	11
Anger	12
Unicorns	13
What Is Normal?	14
Mania	15
Nobody Is Listening	16
My Safe Place	17
I Feel Her Pain	18
Voices Taken	19
Neglected	20
Failure	22
Worst Nightmare	23
No One's Perfect	24
Trust	25

Body Language	26
I Just Want to Fly Away	27
Bipolar	28
Real or Not	29
Someone Help Me	30
It Cannot Break Me	31
Psychologist	32
Pain	33
Silence Is Golden	34
Escape	35
Feelings	36
Jokes in My Head	37
Mute	38
No Need to Rush	39
Good Vibes	40
Friends	41
My Niece	42
Mum	43
So Confused	44
Time to Explore	45
Little Lost Lamb	46
Not Just My Man	47
Mother's Day	48

101 Things	**49**
Mini New York	**50**
Zzzz	**51**
Grateful	**52**
Will I Get Better?	**53**
Dear Lord	**54**
Fly to the Stars	**55**
Precious Childhood	**56**
Beautiful Butterfly	**57**
My Life Is a Mess	**58**
My Boy	**59**
Ssh, Sit Down	**60**
Bad Day	**61**
Choices	**62**
Medication	**63**
No Longer Love Silence	**64**
Sadness	**65**
Scared	**66**
Believe in Yourself	**67**
Hope	**68**
Life's a Struggle	**69**
Angels	**70**
Fear	**71**

Voices	72
When I Am Better	73
My Sister	74
Bro	75

One Wish

If I had one wish then this is what it would be'
I don't ask for much just your honesty.

I don't have much to give in fact only my heart'
It promises not to hurt you or tear you apart.
My heart has taken so much hurt it finds it hard to trust,
But if your heart beats the same as mine loving you is a must.
I cannot try any more than I have, I've tried to help you out,
But you keep hurting me, you make me want to shout!
So this here is my final word I have written in black and white,
If you can't love me the right way please stay out my sight.

A Mother's Love

A mother's love has never been so pure,
Nothing is less I crave more and more.
Their beautiful eyes and loving smiles, make me drift for miles and miles.
Their tight hugs and slobbery kisses, if I didn't have them, something would be missing.
Whenever I am sad, they don't say a word,
Just wrap their arms around me like arms around the world.
Nothing is a better feeling than knowing your kids are near,
and I hope they know that I love them very dear.

Love Hurts

Love hurts, you know, the unconditional kind,
All I want to do is protect my family, but they seem to be blind.
That sickly feeling down deep in my stomach, Everyday it hurts, i'd rather be hit by a bullet.
I stress too much and overanalyse things,
But I'd rather that than have the danger it brings.
Prevention is better than the cure I always say,
But they don't understand, they just want to go and play.
Every siren, every horn, I sit there hoping, praying, " Please no more."
It's not till that moment they walk through the door,
Thank God, that's a better feeling than before.

Anger

Anger is something I hate to feel,
I wish this madness was not real.
My tongue is bitter and something nasty,
The voices keep pushing till people walk past me.
I have lost my family and I have no friends,
Looks like I'm on this roller coaster by myself till the end.
But when is the end? Nobody knows,
Looks like I have to struggle and see where life goes.

Unicorns

Unicorns are not real crazy people are meant to see them,
I have waited a long, long time but I think it's just a dream.

Looking high'
Looking low,
Side to side,
To and fro.
Come out, come out, wherever you are,
They say you can fly; I want to see how far.
I will try again tomorrow,
Same time I will come,
I will bring a treat too,
So please, do not run.

What Is Normal?

Does anyone know?
Anyone who says they are I don't think so.
Everyone has faults but so it goes,
It doesn't mean people should turn up their nose.
Yes, everyone has problems some more than others,
The ones that really need help, nobody bothers.
I said to my CPN: "Unless you have been there, don't tell me you understand."
His reply was "I hope you trust I have enough knowledge and education. US CPNs are in demand."
It helps to know I'm not alone others out there are same,
People are not like me,
They're always looking for someone to blame.

Mania

And there it is again, quick where is my hiding den?
They're coming to get me and time is running out,
Please! Mr. Policeman! hear my shout!
But the policeman said to me: "I'm sorry miss, but no one can help you here, you see."
Once they found out that I was crazy the local authority became very lazy.

I was left in tears and fearing my life'
Bipolar is certainly rife.
Can I beat it? I don't know,
It keeps beating me down testing how far I will go.

Nobody Is Listening

It's true nobody listens to what I have to say'
I can see by the look in their eyes
They think, My God! not again today!
It's true I trust no one what else can I say?
But when I have been hurt so bad, am I silly to still play?
I'm not shy with my love anyone can tell you that,
But when you give too much, they take it for granted and that's also a fact.
I'm best off all alone all I wanted was a life,
My children to be happy and make a good husband and wives.
I keep telling myself life is too short to worry,
All I want is to live my life with my family and always remain jolly.

The doctors just called me, what do I do?
I looked at the door then I looked at him,
Chances of getting out looked very slim.
I went into his room, and I sat down.

"How can I help today? Why such a big frown?
You have had a stressful week,
You are having a manic moment,
Please go home and I will contact a grownup.
I will also let the crisis team know that you were here, please go home and please do not fear."
What if I had wandered off to do something tragic?
They would have covered it up and made it disappear like magic.

Failure

Why do I feel like a failure when I'm trying my best? Will someone tell me how to stop this mess!
Every day is negative, a big cloud over me,
I want sunshine, sunshine shining down on me.
But that's too much to ask my mind doesn't want me to be happy,

It makes me feel bad' and every day is crappy.
I don't understand what this is all about!
Bipolar, mental health is a serious account!
If I could turn back the clock, I would turn it all the way,
And pray so hard I wasn't born that day.

Worst Nightmare

Everyone has a worst nightmare, if mine wasn't so scary I wouldn't care.
But multiply what you feel by a thousand,
If you had what I have, you'd wish you'd never found it.
They say it's just a label but it's way more than that,
If I could find one big enough, I'd hide under a hat.
People like to laugh and stare; I just think how you would feel in your worst nightmare?
Yes, it's shameful and always embarrassing,
It's so out of control I would say it's harassing.
There's no getting away from it' it has total control' I feel like a goldfish living in a bowl.

No One's Perfect

I'm not perfect but I'm also not bad,
To know that people think bad things of me makes me so sad.

I don't look for trouble' more just a friend'
But the people I meet, they just pretend.
Nobody is honest these days, that's certainly changed! I remember good people back in the day.
All they do these days is chat behind your back,
I'm like; "really!" you should cut each other some slack.
I've no time for drama I have enough of my own, why don't they live their own lives?
Afterall…they are supposed to be grown.

Trust

When you're feeling sad and low and think that no one cares,
Just remember that person who is with you when you're scared.
Long scary nights and long scary days,
Not knowing or understanding but they are with you when you pray.
They care so much about you, and I know you don't think so,
But just give that person a chance to help you to grow.
It may not seem like it now, but please, please believe,
Your time is coming and soon you will be free.

Body Language

When I go into mania my body language changes, my daughter looks at me for ages and ages.
"Are you okay, Mum?" she softly says and asks me so many times throughout the day.
I keep telling her I'm fine, I don't want her to worry,
But then it's so powerful, she doesn't want to leave in a hurry.
You can see her pondering, she doesn't want to go to school,
"I just want to stay home Mum, and take care of you."
She goes to care and guidance and cries to her teachers,
"She is so lost miss, I'm trying hard, but I just cannot reach her."
They show her comfort and persuade her to stay,
She replies, "Okay miss, but can you call her and see if she is okay!"

I Just Want to Fly Away

Why do I hurt the people that I love?
Sometimes I want to fly away just like a dove.
It makes me feel bad, in fact rotten,
But all the bad things I said to them seem to be forgotten.
I pull people close, then I push them away, i'm so confused, what more do you want me to say?
I beat myself down almost every day, I hate myself and know one day I will pay.
I get visions all the time of people at my funeral,
I find myself choosing songs and making sure I get a good burial.
Is this going to beat me?
I hope the visions I have are not of near reality.

Bipolar

What is it?
It's a game that plays with your brain.
Some days it can be funny, but others noway.
The manic moments came with laughter and joy,
But some days when it's over the top, I stop and think, Oh boy!
The feeling someone is out to get me has to be the worst, The feeling of dying, I'm on a long road in reverse.
I just want to run, I just want to hide,
But then I remember it's all in my mind.
My heart rate slows, and my brain takes a breath, come on my love, go home and get some rest.
Bipolar is tiring, it drains me to the core,
I just don't want to be here, in this place anymore.

Real or Not

Reality or not? Sometimes I don't know,
All different stuff in my brain, it's in constant flow.
Is this real?
Is that not?
Look how bad my life has got! always checking this and that,
constantly thinking my life has been hacked.
Take a step back and look again,
Sometimes, your eyes, they pretend.
Hallucinations are not really there, why am I telling you this?
It's not like you care.

Someone Help Me

I wish someone could help me,
I'm lost and don't know where to go,
For a long time I have been wandering down this road. No left, no right, just straight on I can go,
I ask them for help, but they tell me: "No, no, no".
There has to be a change somewhere, please, show me the light!
I'm tired of living this life, I'm fighting with all my might!
There is only so much one can take, every day is a battle,
In the end I'm sitting shaking, rattle, rattle, rattle.
When will I be free from fear? I'm asking you for help! I think this has to be the hardest card dealt!
Guide me through all the darkness and pain,
And maybe, just maybe, I can be happy again.

It Cannot Break Me

Bipolar cannot break me, it cannot bring me down,
As bad as my life gets and as much as I frown.
You cannot destroy me; you are all in my head!
I'm going to survive this, it's you that's going to be dead. You have tortured me now for such a long time,
I know I will get better, in the end, victory will be mine. You beat me down every single day,
Thank you for teaching me to keep you at bay.

Psychologist

I walk in her room, and I sit on a chair,
I'm here because I'm about to lay my life bare. None-processed memories just floating around,
These thoughts and feelings need bringing down.
Every day, they flash in my mind, like Hey! I'm still here till the end of time!
She makes me feel relaxed and calm, she said in time I will know there's no harm.
She deliberately brings out my fears,
And tells me when I am over this, I will live on for years. She makes me feel safe and brings me down a level,
And tells me softly no one is the devil.
I know she's going to help me; I will get there in the end, I really have to thank her but please, don't pretend.

Pain

Pain can sometimes hurt like a knife through the heart,
Deeper and deeper it goes and makes sure to leave a scar.
So much hurt, too much pain bolting through me, this is insane!
How long will it last? this feeling of sadness?
It's only a matter of time before it turns to madness.

Then there I am' down deep in this hole'
Wondering where there is for me to go.

Home, home is the place for me'
It's the only place I feel security.

Silence Is Golden

Silence is golden I used to say to myself,
Kids off to school, look! even clean shelves.
Tidying's done, dishes put away, let's pop to the shops and see what they have forme today.
Come back home, put the shopping in the cupboards,
Time to hurry, the children are out mother hubbard!

Come back home and cook the tea'
Whoosh! I'm done! it's bed for me.
Put the kids to bed, then off I go myself,
Make sure to set that alarm up on that shelf.
School tomorrow, same routine, this is the life I loved, right here was me.

Escape

My head is banging I can't think straight,
All these mixed-up feelings, I need to escape.
I'm stuck inside my own mind and thinking too much,
I have got all these things to say but they keep telling me to hush!
Who would believe a word I say? Ha! that I'd like to see!
I know the people who talk behind my back, they say I'm just crazy.
Because I have bipolar, people don't want to believe,
You get pushed out because really, they have pet peeves.
I don't care that 'I'm on my own'
It's probably for the best,
I'm just not the same as all the rest.

Feelings

Feelings have to be the worst thing in the world,
If it's all this and that, then why does it hurt?

I have loved so much and got nothing in return'
Take these feelings and let them burn.
Feelings hurt, no denying that fact,
If I knew then, what I know now, my bag would be packed.
All they do is take, take, take,
You can clearly see this love is fake!
So, why do I keep letting my heart take a beating?
Because I feel like life without him wouldn't be worth living.

Jokes in My Head

They tell me jokes inside my head,
They say it's funny, go tell a friend.
But I just laugh and give a giggle… really?
Are you sure they won't think it's just a riddle?
They are funny I have to say, and when it's like this, I don't mind it lasting for days.
They are the best conversations i've ever had,
I think, finally, I have gone mad!

Mute

When I want to speak the words will not come out,
I really want to say something, I really want to shout!
I wonder why my mouth won't open when I have so much to say?
My brain has had enough, it no longer wants to play.
I'm muted and I can't do a thing, my brain doesn't want me to speak,
So all the things you wanted to know about me, you shall now have to seek.

No Need to Rush

Take your time no need to rush'
I'm just here to guide your push.
You need confidence that's what you need,
You have to find it from somewhere if you want to succeed. I
can only help a little bit the rest is up to you,
Make sure to spread your wings and you will breakthrough.
Never give up and always think positive,
Think of your future, that's your main prerogative.
You will get there, there's so much for you to see,
Your future will be bright, just how you want it to be.

Good Vibes

Good vibes, I need to find some,
Instead of sitting in a world so gruesome.
I'm sick of feeling down all the time,
If I had good vibes, I would be fine.
How can I get some? I really want to know,
If you can please, just tell me, off I will go.
Maybe, if I had good vibes my life wouldn't be so dull,
I wouldn't be sat here constantly like a raging bull.
So please, if you don't mind pointing me the right way,
I can go get myself some good vibes and have a better day.

Friends

I'm constantly inside my own mind,
No friends to talk to, I lost them through time.
Not that I did anything wrong, friends just don't stay around me long.

I prefer to be myself then there's no drama'
I'm a great believer in waiting on karma.
But being alone is not very nice,
I would like a life with a bit of spice.
A couple of friends to talk to and tell secrets,
To have a laugh with and share drinks and pizza.
That would be nice' in fact, that would be great!
For me to finally have a life and some mates.

My Niece

My niece is so special to me I love her so much,
When I'm feeling down, the best thing is feeling her touch.
I may not see her much; I'd love to see her more! She fills my life with love so pure.
She will always hold a place in my heart, so very, very, dear, even when she isn't around, I still feel her near. My door is always open to her no matter what, it doesn't matter how long she's gone, she will never be forgot!

Mum

I'd love to know who invented the word 'mum'?
When someone says it, we turn when it's not even our son.
Too many women, with the same name,
Whoever thought of it must be insane!
Hundreds and hundreds of people, hear the same sound, Hear the word mum, and all turn around.
It's funny but not at the sametime, you turn around thinking every kid is mine,
But in the end, we are all one,
We are the best and should never be frowned upon.

So Confused

My heads so confused and my heart's feeling sad,
I didn't know loving people could make me feel so bad.
I thought loving was happy-ever-after, what a fairytale I live in,
My heart is ready to play but I want to put it in the bin.
It makes me feel sick, I can't eat or sleep,
This feeling of love I have, it goes so deep.
I don't want to feel love anymore, please take it away,
My heart has second thoughts about this and no longer wants to play.

Time to Explore

Just when everything seems alright, I sit up with a jerk and almighty fright.
That horrible feeling is back again; so strong, it's sending me round the bend.
No one listens when I get scared, I'm left all alone, thinking no one cares.
I get left alone inside my own mind,
Same things going around, time after time.
My brain is under pressure, it can't take anymore, why doesn't it take time to explore?
Time to put my life in order, even for just a fraction, I want to enjoy life and feel satisfaction.

Little Lost Lamb

How do I stop caring and giving a damn?
You have me following you like a little lost lamb.
I don't want to go down your road, I want to go down my own,
Because, I know at the end of mine is a big throne. I deserve to sit on it, big and proud,
I got to where I am today, on my own grounds.
No one has really helped me, as they don't understand, my kids tho, they come first in command.
They have been there through the good and bad,
All the times I lashed out and was uncontrollably sad.
Never questioning me or asking me what's wrong,
They all sit around and sing me a song.
A song of love, they sing to me,
"Everything will be okay, Mum, you will see."

Not Just My Man

You're not just my man, you're also my best friend, I knew you wouldn't give up on me in the end.
I know life with me cannot be easy,
I promise I will try, but it's not easy-peasy.
It's not that easy, when it's in a muddle,
The logical side's confused and the emotional in a puddle. I just need time to put my life in order,
To put bad memories behind me, and be able to move forward.
Once I have managed that, things will be great,
Because I knew, all along having you in my life was fate.

Mother's Day

Today is Mother's Day, what can I say?
To me, it's just like any other day.

I never received anything in the past'
I never really wanted Mother's Day to last.
But this year has been different, it's been totally fab, I got flowers and chocolates and more in a bag.
The kids all surrounded me for their kisses,
It was lovely to hold them, that I have been missing.
It's the best Mother's Day I have ever had,
This Mother's Day has been so special, not one thing bad. I have never felt more wanted than I have today,
And they all showed me, in their own special way.

101 Things

Look into my eyes, what do you see?
101 things hurting me.
If you look hard enough, you might see,
The little spark I have left inside of me.
The spark is fading, it's hard for me to see,
Please, someone, rescue me.
I'm seeing life through tinted glass,
I just want to be free at last!
I want to enjoy life and get out of the house,
But when I hit public, I'm like a little mouse. I start to rush, and I panic,
I need to hurry home, before it turns manic!
You don't understand how this makes me feel,
It's so doomed and gloomed, my life doesn't feel real.

Mini New York

My house is a mini–New York, a house that never sleeps, Kids up and down the stairs trying to sneak a peek.
Always think they are missing something, when really there's nothing to see,
I'm sure they like annoying me!
As much as I try, I cannot get angry,

They make me laugh' but always try me.
In the end, our bellies hurt with laughter,
This is the life I long to be after.

Zzzz

I wish I could goto sleep,
I've tried everything, even counting sheep.
But it's no good, my eyes will not close,
I'm too scared to sleep, the kids, who's watching those? I have to protect them; they are part of me,
They are the only thing I love in life and my main priority. I don't know why these feelings are so strong!
What is it I've done that's so wrong?
Why are you making me frantic?
You must think watching me go crazy is fantastic. Please take it away, I don't like it anymore.
I have no fun in life, it's become a total bore.

Grateful

If I give you my heart, do you promise to take care of it? It's abit battered and brushed and been kicked a bit.
It just needs someone to love, someone to feel close to…
I would like to know if that person could be you? It's a happy little heart, that has room to grow,
It really wants to be loved you know!
Give it a chance, and see where it leads,
In the end you will be grateful you took this heart from me.

Will I Get Better?

Will I ever get better? Please answer me'
I'm tired now, physically and emotionally.
My head hurts from all the thinking, it's like my brain is throbbing and cells shrinking.
I'm looking for answers that I cannot find,
I've been looking so hard for a long time!
But then do I know what I'm really searching for? I don't know, but I keep looking for more.
Every day is just the same to me, I wish it could be different, instead of people staying away and keeping their distance.

I just want to get better and make some friends'
Not let this illness control me till the end.

Dear Lord

Dear Lord please hear my cry,
What is it that I've done so wrong for me to want to die?
I wake up every day, feeling nothing but pain, pain stabbing me again and again!
I look hard but I cannot see,
I'm asking you now, please help me!
I need guidance and I need light,
I'm giving it my best, but I am losing this fight. I'm not strong enough on my own,
Please watch over me, and protect my home.
Protect my children, let them come to no harm,
Always stay beside them, from night till dawn.
They are so precious, they mean everything to me,
Take care of them, protect them, and I will give my soul for free.

Fly to the Stars

Take my hand come fly with me,
I'll take you to the stars, wait and see!
Everything is so pretty and twinkling so bright,
Being there when you need someone, feels so right.
Stars flashing pink, purple and blue, look they are twinkling just for you!
If you like, you can catch one in ajar, take it home and keep it in your heart.
Whenever you feel down, just hold it tight,
And it will twinkle to show you everything is all right. Life's not that bad you know, you will see,
You shine as bright as the star you hold on your knee.

Precious Childhood

Your childhood is precious don't let anyone steal this, even if they tell you, they really didn't mean it.
They make you feel special, and show you attention,
But the bad things they have in mind, they forget to mention.
They buy you things to make themselves look good,
But keep what they do to you under their hood.
Don't be fooled by people who pretend to be nice,
Doing bad things to you does not give them the right.

Keep yourself safe' and just so you know,
You absolutely have the right to say no.

Beautiful Butterfly

I wish I was a butterfly fluttering in the sky'
Look, look at me! I'm flying so high!
Looking down on an endangered world, I look and think, oh how this has turned.
I would be pleased not to be part of it, no right to be free, there will always be someone, somewhere, wanting to control me.
Being a butterfly, you go wherever you want,
Flying at a level you know you won't get harmed. Fluttering here, fluttering there,
So, so, happy, not one single care.
Oh, how I'd love to be a butterfly, next time maybe, I might push out my shell, beautiful and free.

My Life Is a Mess

What shall I do? My life is such a mess,
I can't do this anymore, I can't stand the stress. My brain is battered and I don't know what to do, I need help and I need it from you.

I feel all alone and it's dark down here,
Please let me out, my life's a big smear.
I don't want to be alone anymore,
Why is this happening to me?
Is it all in my mind? I'm not sure you see.
I know one day it will break me and I can't get that out of my head,
One day, someone will wake up and find me dead in my bed.
Don't say I didn't tell you so,
You thought that I was fine,
When all I ever wanted, was for someone to be mine.

My Boy

I had four girls before my son was born,
If I didn't have him, then I would have had more.
But I got him in the end, and I am pleased,
Anymore pregnancies would have broken me!
He's so loving, he is my prince,
I loved him the day he was born, and I've loved him ever since.

He tells me he loves me before he goes to bed'
He kisses my cheek and he kisses my head.
He is the best; I couldn't ask for more,
He's the No.1 man in my life, the one I adore.

Ssh, Sit Down

Ssh, come here, there's no need to shake,
Please, sit down and tell me the reason for your quake.
You look all flushed and, in a hurry,
Is there really any need for you to scurry!?
Sit yourself down and have a minute,
I'm right here if you want me to listen.
It doesn't matter how good or bad,
To help make you feel better would make me so glad.
So come on my love, what's going on?
Sharing with two hearts is better than one.

Bad Day

It was a bad day' and I didn't want to be here'
Spending all day with the ones I love dear.
Knowing inside what I was going to do,
But the voices said, "Keep it between me and you, we will do it when they have gone,
don't worry, it won't take long."
When they were gone, I sat at the table,
All these tablets, was I really able?
Yes, I was and down they went,
It wasn't long before the ambulance was sent.

Four and a half hours in resuscitation'
To believe, I did this without hesitation!
So many faces crying over me,
You can't do this again, Nikki, please!

Choices

Why are choices so hard to make?
How do you make one with so much at stake? Do I, or don't I? That is the question,
I have to think twice before I give it a mention.
Why can't I make a choice?
What's wrong with me?
All I ever come out with is, "Okay, we will see."
I wish that I was able and strong, to know the choices I wanted to make were not wrong.
But I can't make choices, looks like I'm stuck here for a while
Stewing, living my life in total denial.

Medication

Medication, is it helpful?
I'm not sure you know,
I take what I take, but it doesn't make it go.
Daytime meds do their job, and keep my mood stable,
If I didn't take them every day, then I would not be able, to clean my home, take care of my kids and put their stuff away,
I'd lay around on the sofa and do nothing at all, all day.
Nighttime meds are not so clever, still feels like I'm awake forever and ever.
Antipsychotics don't do a thing, the voices are always there leaving their string.
Good or bad, nasty or evil, I really can't stand anymore upheaval.

No Longer Love Silence

I no longer love silence, it's thinking time,
Over and over it plays in my mind.

They are coming, they are coming,
They keep shouting at me,
I keep looking back but I cannot see.
I close my blinds and lock my door,
If I hide down here, they won't come anymore.
But it's no good, they are ripe in my head,
I'm so sick of this now, I wish I was dead.

Sadness

Sadness is so dark and blue,
If you could feel the pain, you would wish it wasn't happening to you.
Always in the dark, remaining all alone, me and sadness are like a pro.
Feeling weak and no interest in life,
To say it's terrible is being polite, no feeling of happiness, no feeling of joy,
No laughter or fun, just sadness that destroys.
Sadness is so sad and blue,
I wish I could take it away, from me and you.

Scared

I'm just so scared,
This life I've been given, I was not prepared.

Please' let me go back and start again'
I know I will get there in the end.
I promise to right all my wrongs, just take this illness and let it be gone.
I will be the best you want me to be,
I will make you proud for all to see!
Just take me back and let me start again,
The life I see in front of me, I don't want, and I won't pretend.

Believe in Yourself

Always believe in yourself, even if others don't,
Don't let them bring you down and make you give up hope.

Always try your best and always push yourself'
You don't belong up on that shelf!
Let yourself go and get yourself noticed,
Your life will be better, and in much better focus. Enjoy yourself and let your spirit be free,
You will rise and rise taller than the trees.
Everyone can be someone, all it takes is courage, your life will thrive and finally nourish!

Go and enjoy yourself, life is way too short'
Oh boy! what a life you have scored.

Hope

Hope is something I wish I had every day,
I wish it would come and take this feeling of pain. My bellies in knots and I can't get them out,
It really doesn't matter how much I scream and shout. That feeling of sickness, right up in my throat,
How many times do I have to be told?
I hope one day I learn my lesson,
Keep wishing for hope is kind of depressing.

Life's a Struggle

Life's a struggle that's for sure,
I keep thinking I can't take anymore.
I'm constantly trying to please other people,
Yet, I'm always the one getting squashed like a beetle. I say
to myself, "Just don't care anymore."
But if I did that, life would be a bore.
I have children and never ask for help,
I do what I do, and I do it myself.
One thing I can certainly say,
I get stronger and stronger every day.

Angels...

I have one, I feel him when he's near,
He's staying by my side, keeping my life in gear.
Everytime I seem to slip, he lifts my wings and says, "No, not yet young lady, you're still in early days!
You have so much to look forward to, please don't give up, it really won't be long, and your life will be in triumph!
We all get tested, that's why we are here,
But it's how we cope with it that makes us very dear,
So, take these words, you hear me say and keep them in your heart,
God, said, 'Don't give up, your life's only about to start.'"

Fear

Worst thing about fear,
Is that it's always lingering so very near.
Creeping up all dull and nasty,
Quick, let me hide, see if it goes past me.
But it clings on tight and lets you know it's there, come on now, please, is this really fair?
I had you yesterday and the day before that,
Can't you please for once just cut me some slack? I'm well aware of the fact that you're there,
But today you see, I really don't care.

Voices

They say the voices are my own thoughts and feelings, it's hard to believe I'd bring myself these dealings.
What are they?
Why are they there?
Why am I living my life in despair?

There has to be reason and logic to this'
What is it!?
Please tell me! what did I miss?
You are constantly nagging me, trying to get arise, I know what you are doing, you want me to die.
But someone once told me, hold on to the truth,
When somebody hurts you, it doesn't always run smooth. It's not your fault, you are not to blame,
Anyone in my position would tell you the same.

When I Am Better

One day when I'm better, I want to help people like me,
Because I want them to understand I see what they see. I think knowing that they would open up a little,
To know someone has lived through it and life is not so brutal.
It takes such a long time to learn to trust,
And honesty, is most certainly, an absolute must!
If you don't have that, then you don't stand a chance, they won't give you a look, let alone a glance.
If you want inside their minds, then you need to be true,
Because if you do that, you will find they open up to you.

My Sister

My beautiful sister, what can I say?
You're elegant and classy in every way.
Ten years between us, it seems so far apart,
But I've loved you from the beginning with all my heart.
You're always there when I need someone,
Someone who understands, never say I'm lying or lay down demands.
You quietly listen to what I have to say,
And sometimes, I see you keeping your tears at bay.
I've said so many horrible things and upset you to the core, I wish I could take back the hurt and promise you no more. I'm sorry for hurting your feelings, and I want you to know, I never meant all the things I said to you, my love for you still grows.

Bro

My brother has become part of the furniture,
Around every day, making sure nobody hurts us. He doesn't say much, just sits watching his phone, Stops, now and again for a coffee and smoke.
He has a bit of convo now and again,
I have to say, he is not just my brother, he is also my best friend. Always got my back no matter what,
Even when my temper becomes very hot!
He has seen me fight a few demons through time, but every day, he is back at mine.
I'm so pleased he is around,
He's picked me up a few times when I've fallen to the ground.
I thank him very much for always being there,
For understanding me, not doubting me and giving me his care.

Printed in Great Britain
by Amazon

37411044R00046